P9-CLX-684

J 320.938 GAG
Gagne, Tammy.
The evolution of government and
politics in the Greece /
EXET

EXET

EXET
FEB 2015

The Evolution of
Government and
Politics in the

GREECE

GREECE

Parliament Building,
Athens, Greece

Tammy Gagne

Tulare County Library

Mitchell Lane

PUBLISHERS
P.O. Box 196
Hockessin, DE 19707

Mitchell Lane
PUBLISHERS

The Evolution of
Government &
Politics

The Evolution of Government and Politics in

CHINA
EGYPT
FRANCE
GERMANY
GREECE
IRAQ
ITALY
NORTH AND SOUTH KOREA
THE UNITED KINGDOM
VENEZUELA

Copyright © 2015 by Mitchell Lane
Publishers Inc.

All rights reserved. No part of this book may
be reproduced without written permission
from the publisher. Printed and bound in
the United States of America.

PUBLISHER'S NOTE: The facts in this book
have been thoroughly researched.
Documentation of such research can be
found on pages 44–45. While every possible
effort has been made to ensure accuracy, the
publisher will not assume liability for
damages caused by inaccuracies in the data,
and makes no warranty on the accuracy of
the information contained herein.
The Internet sites referenced herein were
active as of the publication date. Due to the
fleeting nature of some web sites, we cannot
guarantee that they will all be active when
you are reading this book.

Printing 1   2   3   4   5   6   7   8   9

Library of Congress
Cataloging-in-Publication Data

Gagne, Tammy.
 The evolution of government and politics in
Greece / by Tammy Gagne.
    pages cm. — (The evolution of
government and politics)
 Audience: Grade 4 to 8.
 Includes bibliographical references and
index.
 ISBN 978-1-61228-584-9 (library bound)
1. Greece--Politics and government—To 146
B.C.—Juvenile literature. 2. Greece—Politics
and government—Juvenile literature. I. Title.
 DF215.G26 2015
 320.938—dc23
                                        2014006938

eBook ISBN: 9781612286211

                                              PBP

Contents

CHAPTER 1

A Greek Tragedy

It was November of 2011, and Greece was in serious financial trouble. Prime Minister George Papandreou had done everything he could to help solve the enormous problems confronting the country—with one exception. Now it was time for that final move. After three days of talks among Greece's political parties, Papandreou announced that he would step down as leader, only halfway through his four-year term. He knew that Greece needed a new government if there was any hope of avoiding bankruptcy—and expulsion from the European Union (EU), an economic and political union of 28 countries.

He explained his decision to the people of Greece in his farewell speech. "It was obvious that in order to achieve this historic agreement, we would have to find a person who had everyone's support," he said. "I believe this choice is very important. My role would never be an obstacle to this national unity."[1]

Greek Prime Minister George Papandreou addresses his nation via television on November 9, 2011, to announce his resignation. Both his father and grandfather had held the same office. Papandreou had been born in Minnesota before moving to Greece as a young man and entering politics.

The last few years had been especially difficult for Greece. Because the country was spending so much, its government had borrowed large amounts of money from other nations. This practice is not uncommon. The total amount a country owes to other nations is called its national debt. The problem was that Greece had borrowed far more money than it could afford to pay back.

When the European Union realized how serious the problem had become, it stepped in to help Greece. The financial crisis that Greece was facing had the potential of becoming a problem for other EU nations if Greece defaulted on its loans.

To make the situation a bit easier to understand, for a moment think of Greece as one of your classmates at school. Let's call him Greg. And think of the EU as your class. Greg's parents give him lunch money each week, but this time he spent all of it on trading cards on Monday. Greg asks you if he can borrow $2.50 for lunch. You lend him the money, and he promises to pay you back on Friday when he gets his allowance. He says he will even buy you a cookie to make the loan worth your effort.

When Friday comes around, you need the cash you loaned Greg to buy your ticket to the school dance. Unfortunately, he hasn't done his chores this week, so his parents do not give him his allowance. You have $2.50 left from your own allowance, but the ticket costs $5.00. Lucky for you, your friend Sam offers to loan you the money you need. You, however, must pay her back the following week—and give her the cookie that Greg had promised to give you. Greg promises that he will get caught up on his chores by that time and pay you back.

When next Friday comes around, though, he still doesn't have the money he owes you. Looking a bit guilty, he invites you to come over after school to play the expensive new video game that you and all your friends have been wanting. Clearly, Greg could not afford the game. But he still bought it, even though he owed you money.

Now you owe Sam $2.50 and a cookie. You also find out that you aren't the only person who has loaned Greg cash. Since the school year began, he has borrowed lunch money from several other classmates. And he promised each of them a cookie as well. In all, he owes his classmates $30 and a dozen cookies.

In this situation, the cookies represent the interest that Greece owes the other nations that have loaned it money. Each of these countries may have to figure out how it will pay its own expenses without repayment from Greece. Like Greg, Greece had been living beyond its means, spending more money than it had—and more than it could afford to keep borrowing.

The European Union wanted Greece to solve its financial problems, so the country could start paying back its debts. The partnership had two choices. It could help Greece with its money problems, or it could kick Greece out of the EU. Countries to which Greece owed large amounts of money wanted Greece to get back on its feet even more than the others. In this case France, Germany, and the United Kingdom (UK) had the most at stake. Countries that had not loaned Greece money had less to lose by removing Greece from the partnership. But they too might be affected if Greece defaulted. This situation could cause these countries to lose money from nations to which they had loaned money.

If this complicated problem wasn't handled just right, it could lead to recession throughout Europe. As Angela Merkel, the chancellor of Germany, pointed out, "Countries in Europe—particularly the countries in the eurozone [18 EU countries which use the euro as their common currency]—are so closely integrated that every serious decision in one capital has effects on the other countries."[2]

The bailout plan that the European Union came up with made it possible for Greece to reduce the amount of its debt. Under the agreement, the nation would have to pay back only 50 percent of the money it owed. The EU also agreed to loan the nation $140 billion in rescue loans to help avoid defaulting—as long as Greece accepted all the bailout conditions.[3]

As much as they wanted Greece to succeed, France, Germany, and the UK knew that helping Greece came with a certain amount

French President Nicolas Sarkozy and German Chancellor Angela Merkel discuss the Greek financial crisis during a meeting of the leaders of the European Union in June 2011. Their countries were among those with the most at stake in the situation.

of risk. What if the European Union came to Greece's rescue with more loans and the country still defaulted? As Nicolas Sarkozy, then the president of France, explained, "We want to continue with the Greeks but there are rules and it's unacceptable that these rules are not followed."[4]

Before he resigned, George Papandreou said that he saw the repayment of the country's debts as vital to its future. He declared, "I believe it's crucial that we show the world that we can live up to our obligations."[5] Papandreou and the rest of the Greek government had to focus on solving the problems that lay before them. But the EU also had to consider how Greece had gotten into this terrible mess.

The country's overspending had actually begun many years earlier. Many people fault Papandreou's socialist party for the crisis. Known as PASOK, it was founded by Papandreou's father Andreas in 1974. But PASOK wasn't the only party that had governed Greece since then. Both PASOK and New Democracy, the other main party in Greece, had made one bad decision after another since Greece had joined the EU in 1981. When reform was needed, the government continued to borrow money. Even worse, it didn't follow through with its commitments to repay its debt. Over and over, the government made promises that it didn't keep.

Some people blame the countries and private banks that continued to loan money to Greece. After all, they made the problem worse every time they extended more credit to the struggling nation. But many Greeks in high positions were dishonest about how much debt the country had. It is hard to say how many people knew exactly how bad the situation was until it was too late.

When Greece won the privilege of hosting the 2004 Olympic Games, the country had fresh hope for getting back on track. But the Games that took place in Athens that year turned into another striking example of overspending. The country paid nearly $11 billion—twice the amount of money it had budgeted for the event. And this staggering amount doesn't even include what was spent on road work and other infrastructure costs. Many projects were completed in a hurry in the final months. Those short deadlines made it necessary for crews to work 24 hours a day. This schedule led to costly overtime wages and the expense of extra electricity for lights during nighttime hours.

To make matters even worse, the Olympic village built to house the athletes quickly turned into a ghost town, rather than providing homes for Greek people. Most of the sports facilities have barely been used since 2004. Even when opportunities to make money with them arose, it seemed that Greece wasn't interested.

Dan Porter is the president of the International Softball Federation. His organization offered to pay the expense of maintaining the softball venue so it could be used for events in the region. But he said no one ever responded to his offer to make a deal. "The softball venue is still standing," he said, "except that it is overgrown with weeds, unmaintained and unused."[6] Like many people around the world, Porter realizes that the problems began long before Greece hosted the games. "Of course it is not only the Olympics that caused Greece's current problems but it probably added to it,"[7] he pointed out.

Indeed, public spending in Greece began soaring long before the Olympic torch arrived in Athens. Between 1999 and 2007, wages controlled by the government rose 50 percent. This increase was much higher than that of other countries within the eurozone. At the same time, Greece was borrowing more and more money—and keeping a big secret. The eurozone places a limit on how much money its members can borrow. A country's total government debt cannot be more than 60 percent of its gross

The broadcast rights, sponsorship and licensing programs, and ticket sales for the 2004 Olympics brought in 2.2 billion dollars (1.69 billion euros).[8] But the expenses were far higher.

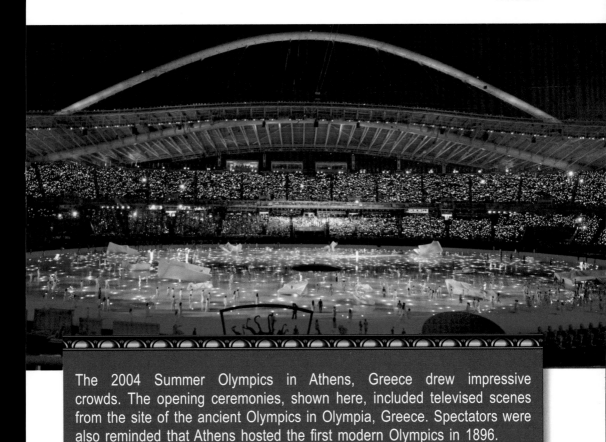

The 2004 Summer Olympics in Athens, Greece drew impressive crowds. The opening ceremonies, shown here, included televised scenes from the site of the ancient Olympics in Olympia, Greece. Spectators were also reminded that Athens hosted the first modern Olympics in 1896.

domestic product (GDP). This is the value of all the goods produced and services provided by that nation in a single year. Greece's debt is currently about 190 percent of its GDP.[9]

The problems that Greece was facing had been building for many years. And the situation was undeniably grim. But it certainly wasn't the first time that Greece had found itself in difficult circumstances.

The International Monetary Fund (IMF) predicts that Greece's GDP will grow by 3 percent each year from 2014 to 2018.[10]

CHAPTER 2

The Birth of Democracy

Greece has one of the world's oldest and most influential governments. In fact, the country is credited with creating the system of democracy on which many modern governments are based. Democracy in Greece can be traced back to 507 BCE, when a nobleman in Athens named Cleisthenes instituted what was known as "demokratia."[1] It meant "rule by the people," and it offered the Athenian people something they had never had before: equality. Until that time Greece had been governed very differently.

For centuries, most Greeks had been ruled by aristocrats. These wealthy people were considered the most important members of society. Their high social standing put them in positions of power. This type of government in which a small number of rich and powerful men make all the decisions is called an oligarchy. Sometimes a single man rose to power. He was called a tyrant, though he usually had the support of many of the people he ruled.

The first person to represent the commercial class—or merchants—in Athenian politics was Cleon. He is depicted in an engraving by 20th century artist William Spencer Bagdatopoulos as he addresses his fellow citizens. He also served as an army general in the Peloponnesian War and was killed in battle in 422 BCE.

Around 700 BCE, ancient Greece was made up of many different areas called city-states. Mountains and large bodies of water served as natural boundaries between these areas. The city-states acted like tiny countries. Each one had its own government. Most of these city-states, like Athens and Sparta, were ruled by oligarchies. Each one had its own military and at least one fortified area that it could use to defend itself against the others if necessary.

The city-state of Sparta was ruled by two kings who served simultaneously, though their power was limited by a 28-member Council of Elders, whose members served lifelong terms. Sparta was one of the most warlike Greek societies. Its fighting men spent much of their time training for combat, as this scene indicates. Spartan women were among the most free in ancient Greece. They could own property and compete in athletics.

Starting in the mid-560s BCE, a man named Pisistratus was the tyrant of Athens. Many people praised him for the way he ran the government. Athens became especially prosperous; he cut the taxes that many people had to pay and made advances in the arts. When he died in 528, his sons Hipparchus and Hippias replaced him and continued many of their father's policies. But Hipparchus was assassinated in 514, which led to a confusing political situation in Athens for several years. Finally Cleisthenes, who had been in exile, returned and took over the city's leadership. He reorganized the way in which the city was governed, giving power to many more people than his predecessors. Most people regard this as the birth of democracy.

It is important to understand that the democracies of ancient Greece did not provide the type of equality that democracies provide today. By the middle of the fifth century BCE, for example, Athens had a total population of about 260,000 people. But at this time someone was considered a citizen only if his or her parents had also been Athenian citizens. The 10,000 or so people who had immigrated to Athens from other areas were not considered citizens. Nor were the slaves, who might have totaled as many as 150,000. Neither the immigrants and slaves nor women and anyone

Cleisthenes is often called the father of Greek democracy. After instituting his reforms in 507 BCE, he disappeared from the pages of history.

under the age of 18 had a say in the new democratic government. As a result, only about 40,000 adult male citizens had voting rights.[2]

Still, the movement towards democracy was historic. In Athens the early democratic government was made up of three main parts. The *ekklesia* was the assembly. The group of male citizens with voting rights was referred to as the *demos*. Each member of the *demos* had the right to attend meetings of the *ekklesia*. It met about 40 times each year at a natural auditorium called the Pnyx. The vast majority of these men could not attend the meetings due to other obligations. Some were too far away, serving in the military. Others could not take the time away from work, as they needed money to support their families. It's likely that only about 5,000 people attended *ekklesia* sessions.

Together these men created new laws, revised existing ones, and made decisions regarding war and foreign policy. Occasionally, they also voted on whether a public official should be ostracized.

Slavery was common in ancient Greece. This vase painting from the 6th century BCE shows a slave carrying large jars called amphorae.

This act, which condemned a person's behavior, expelled him from Athens for a period of 10 years. Of course, not everyone agreed about these matters. Before any decisions were made, the group would vote. Whatever the majority wanted was what the *ekklesia* would do.

The *boule* was another governing body. It was different from the *ekklesia* in several ways. Also called the Council of Five Hundred, the *boule* consisted of only 500 men. Cleisthenes had divided Athens into ten tribes. Fifty men from each tribe represented the group in the *boule*, each for a one-year term.

One of the biggest responsibilities of the *boule* was to decide which matters were important enough to put before the *ekklesia*. It also determined if potential officeholders were fit to serve, by asking questions about the candidate's family, treatment of parents, military status, and so on. Because of its responsibilities, the *boule* met daily. Its role was to manage the day-to-day business of the government. Its members supervised other members of the government. It also saw to it that the army and navy ran smoothly, getting the things they needed. When ambassadors from other areas visited Athens, members of the *boule* would meet with them.

Those who served in the *boule* were chosen by a lottery system of sorts. The Athenians insisted that choosing individuals to serve on the *boule* this way was actually more democratic than voting. In theory, this process assured the people that individuals could not buy their way onto the council with either money or charm. It also prevented *boule* members from holding seats on the council for numerous terms in a row. Today the term we use for individuals who do this is career politicians. Unfortunately, the lotteries did not always appoint a completely new group of

> The ten tribes of Athens were named for local heroes. They included Erechthesis, Aegeis, Pandianis, Leontis, Acamantis, Oeneis, Cecropis, Hippothontis, Aeantis, and Antiochis.

councilors. In fact, the high number of wealthy men who were chosen has caused many people to suspect that the system was not always as honest as the government made it seem.

The third and final part of the ancient Greek government was its justice system, known as the *dikasteria*. Greece had no police force at this time. When laws were broken, the *demos* took the matters to the *dikasteria*. The *demos* would then argue the cases for both the prosecution and defense, as lawyers do in U.S. courts today. Each day 500 jurors were chosen from the *demos* to hear the cases and vote on them. Jurors had to be male and at least 30 years of age. A simple majority decided the verdicts.

Like the other parts of the ancient Greek government, the *dikasteria* worked very differently than the courts of modern democracies. For one thing, virtually any case could be brought in front of the *dikasteria*. As a result, many trivial cases ended up being heard. Some cases were brought about simply to embarrass or punish the enemies of the people who brought them.

One thing that this ancient court did have in common with the courts we have today was the way jurors were compensated for their service. People who served as jurors for the *dikasteria* were paid for their time, just like modern jurors are. The reason for this compensation was to prevent juries from being made up of only wealthy citizens who could afford to take time away from work. But also like our modern government, the *dikasteria* paid its jurors less than what they would earn from working. Many jurors ended up being older citizens who had already retired from working. A young person was unlikely to be judged by a jury of his peers—a right given to all citizens of the United States today.

Despite the progress Athens had made, democracy would not remain the country's system of government. During the middle of the fifth century BCE, a general named Pericles came into power. He brought Athens into what is known as its Golden Age.

Probably the most famous case the *dikasteria* ever decided involved the famous Athenian philosopher Socrates. He was found guilty of the charges brought against him and sentenced to death by drinking poisonous hemlock.

CHAPTER 3

The Golden Ruler

Pericles was elected *strategos*, a type of general, in 460 BCE. A member of a wealthy family, he was related to Cleisthenes. Pericles deeply believed in the reforms that Cleisthenes had set in motion. As *strategos*, Pericles worked to continue those reforms.

He also cared deeply about making Athens a center for arts and culture. During his 30 years as leader, Pericles was behind the creation of many brilliant pieces of architecture, most notably the Parthenon. This was a temple dedicated to the worship of the goddess Athena and was located on the Acropolis, the city's highest point. Some of the most talented sculptors and playwrights of this era were among his friends. Pericles wanted their work to be enjoyed by all, not just the wealthy. He made sure that a certain number of tickets to performances of plays were set aside for people who could not afford to buy them. He was also the driving force behind paying jurors for their service.

This statue of Pericles, created in 1833, stands in the Tuileries Garden in Paris. Its title is "Pericles distributing crowns to artists" and symbolizes his importance in creating some of the most beautiful structures in Athens, especially the Parthenon.

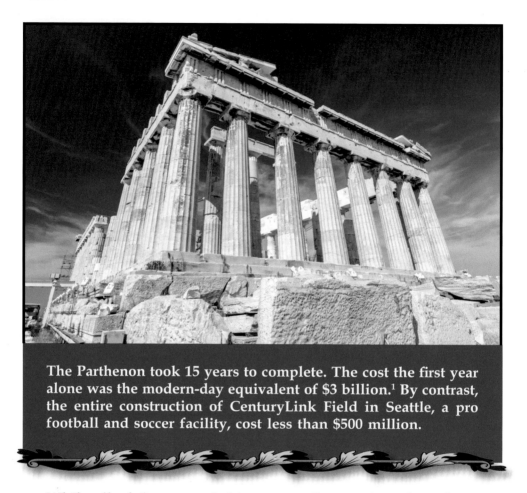

The Parthenon took 15 years to complete. The cost the first year alone was the modern-day equivalent of $3 billion.[1] By contrast, the entire construction of CenturyLink Field in Seattle, a pro football and soccer facility, cost less than $500 million.

While all of these good things were happening, though, some bad things were also going on in Greece. During Pericles's childhood, Persia had set out to conquer Greece not just once, but twice. Both times the Greeks had prevailed. But this would not be the end of war for the country.

Ironically, the very way that Pericles assumed power sparked the beginning of the end for democracy in Athens. In 461, he and his associates had set forth a vote in the assembly that took the power away from the old council of nobles. The nobles were not happy about this turn of events. Shortly after the nobles were removed from power, one of Pericles' top associates, a man named Ephialtes, was assassinated. Once again Athens was in the midst of much turmoil.

The Athenian leader Cimon saw all this unrest as an opportunity. He decided to try to take over as leader. But the Athenians saw him as someone who opposed democracy and ostracized him. This move paved the way for Pericles to lead the people. Many others would challenge Pericles in his new position.

One of them was Thucydides, a former Olympic wrestler who was related to Cimon. Thucydides tried everything he could think of to turn the Athenian people against Pericles. But he failed. Pericles was a master orator who was also known for his honesty. Thucydides tried to imply that his rival's talents for speaking had more to do with persuasion than truth. "If I wrestle him to the ground he will deny this," he declared, "and deny it so vigorously that he will convince even those who witnessed the fight."[2] The people didn't believe him. Years later, he was ostracized.

Pericles would remain in power for many years. Because he was a just ruler, the people did not suffer under his leadership. But they also didn't gain power in the form of a fuller democracy. He was the one making most of the decisions for the country. A famous historian, also named Thucydides, summed it up this way: "In name democracy, but in fact the rule of one man."[3]

Perhaps Pericles' rival—the wrestler Thucydides—had a point. It did seem that Pericles could talk the people of Athens into almost anything. In 431, he even talked them into going to war with Sparta. The conflict became known as the Peloponnesian War, and it pitted Athens and the city-states

This statue of historian/general Thucydides stands outside the Austrian parliament building in Vienna.

23

Athenian naval forces defeat a fleet of ships from Sparta and its allies in 429 BCE, early in the Peloponnesian War. Even though the Athenians were outnumbered, they used superior tactics to win the battle. They captured a number of enemy vessels without any losses of their own.

who supported it against Sparta and its allies. At first it seemed the campaign was going to be a successful one. Athens had many advantages, the biggest of these being its large navy. What neither Pericles nor the people expected, however, was losing more than 20 percent of the city's population to a different enemy: sickness.

Ships that carried food into Athens brought a devastating plague with them. At a time when the soldiers and sailors had to be at their strongest to win the war, they were dying left and right from this illness. In all more than 20,000 people were lost to the plague. Within a year Pericles himself would become one of the victims.[4]

His death didn't bring an end to the war. Without their beloved leader, the Athenians couldn't seem to turn his strategies into consistent victories. The Spartans defeated the Athenians at the Battle of Mantinea in 418. Athens took the island of Melos in 416. But an invasion of the city of Syracuse on the island of Sicily was a disaster for Athens, which lost thousands of fighting men by the time the fighting ended in 413. Athens finally surrendered to Sparta nine years later.

The Spartans quickly installed a government in Athens known in history as the rule of the Thirty Tyrants. The Athenians did not accept the return of an oligarchy without a fight, however. At first their protests were not tolerated, and more than 1,500 Athenians were killed for demanding democracy.[5] The remaining supporters of democracy realized that they needed to become more organized. For a brief period, they left Athens. When they returned, they defeated the tyrants. Some of the tyrants were killed; others fled. Greece was once again a democracy.

Scientists now believe that the illness that killed Pericles and 20,000 of his fellow Athenians was typhoid fever.[6]

CHAPTER 4

Centuries of Changes

Greece's city-states had a long history of fighting among one another. The sixth-century BCE storyteller Aesop is credited with the popular phrase "United we stand; divided we fall."[1] It means that any group that suffers from infighting is likely to be defeated by its enemies. If only the city-states of Greece had listened to this warning. Their constant battles among one another following the Peloponnesian War allowed King Philip II of Macedon, a kingdom in northeastern Greece, to conquer them in 338 BCE.

Next, Philip wanted to conquer one of Greece's biggest enemies: Persia. But Philip was assassinated in 336, leaving his son Alexander to finish his ambition. Alexander the Great, as he would be known in history, did just that in 331. He also added Egypt to his growing empire. Then he headed eastward, eventually going as far as modern-day India.

As a result of Alexander's conquests, Greek culture spread over a wide expanse of territory. This

ΦΙΛΙΠΠΟΣ Β'
ΒΑΣΙΛΕΥΣ ΜΑΚΕΔΟΝΩΝ

Phillip II became king of Macedon in 359 BCE. He gradually conquered the other regions of Greece and took full control in 338. He planned on invading Persia but was assassinated in 336.

This 1736 painting by Italian artist Placido Costanzi depicts Alexander the Great consulting with Dinocrates, his chief architect, as they make plans for the establishment of the city of Alexandria, Egypt. It was commissioned by King Philip V of Spain for his throne room. Many European rulers liked to associate themselves with Alexander.

> Many people now consider Alexander the Great one of the greatest military leaders of all time. But in his own lifetime, he wasn't admired nearly as much. His bad temper and his habit of drinking too much made many ancient Greeks downright despise him.[2]

period of history is known as the Hellenistic Age. People in Alexandria, the city in Egypt that Alexander named for himself, spoke *koine*. This common Greek dialect could also be heard in other places throughout the empire.

The Hellenistic Age would outlive Alexander, who died in 323 BCE, by nearly 300 years. Like Greek democracy, Hellenism— as it was known—would also have many lasting effects on the surrounding lands. Greece, Persia, and Egypt would return to their separateness following Alexander's death. But Greek culture—from its language to its art—would remain part of these and many other nations to this day.

The chances are good that you don't speak Greek. But you know more about the language than you realize. All you have to do is pick up a dictionary to see how many English words have Greek etymologies, referring to the origins of words. Words such as athlete, bicycle, and chorus come from the Greek language. So do thousands of others.

In 146 BCE, Greece came under Roman rule. Over the course of many succeeding centuries, Greece had other rulers. Starting in 1453, Greece came under the control of the Ottoman Turks. In 1821, the Greeks revolted. Aided by Great Britain, France, and Russia, they defeated the Ottomans 11 years later in what is known as the Greek War of Independence. In 1896 the first modern Olympic Games were held in Athens. The last time the event occurred had been in the late fourth century CE. Greece was slowly reclaiming the wonderful things that made it such an incredible place in ancient times.

Elaborately costumed Greek soldiers called *efzones* parade in Athens on March 25, which Greeks celebrate as their independence day. It falls on the anniversary of the start of the Greek War of Independence in 1821.

Greece continued its battles with the Turks into the 20th century. The Balkan Wars that took place in 1912 and 1913 helped Greece reclaim two more areas—southern Macedonia and the island of Crete. In 1924, the people voted to abolish the monarchy that had been established when Greece became independent. The country became a republic at this time. But just a bit more than a decade later, the monarchy was restored.

During World War II, Greece came under German control and underwent a brutal occupation. The Germans withdrew in 1944 and British forces moved in. At this time, Georgios Papandreou—George Papandreou's grandfather—took office as prime minister. Fighting wasn't entirely behind Greece even then, however. A civil war raged from 1946 to 1949. In 1952, the country ratified a new constitution, making it a kingdom governed by a parliamentary democracy.

Greece still had many changes ahead. The Greek military seized power in 1967 and ruled for seven years. In 1974, Greece

These infantry officers served in the Balkan Wars of 1912 and 1913. Greece joined Bulgaria, Serbia, and Montenegro in fighting against the Ottoman Empire. Greece nearly doubled in size as its acquisitions included southern Macedonia and the island of Crete.

High-ranking German officers tour the Acropolis in Athens, soon after the German army defeated Greek forces in April 1941. The resulting German occupation lasted for three and a half years and was especially brutal. Hundreds of thousands of Greeks died of starvation or were executed.

became a republic once again and also voted to abolish the monarchy. At this time Konstantinos Karamanlis became the prime minister. The following year, the country ratified another new constitution. This one stated that the nation would now be a parliamentary republic with some executive powers given to a president. In 1981, Georgios Papandreou's son Andreas—who in turn was the father of the 21st century prime minister George Papandreou—became prime minister. He oversaw the process by which Greece joined the European Union that year.

Twenty years later, in 2001, Greece became part of the eurozone. That means it stopped using the drachma, which had been its system of money for many years. Greece replaced the drachma with the euro, a currency which more than a dozen European countries now use. Three years later the government said it had lied about its budget in order to get into the eurozone. The European Commission issued the country a formal warning at that time. The country was clearly in deep trouble.

Despite the dire financial crisis that soon became apparent to the rest of the world, Greece's government has continued on. Today it consists of three branches: executive, legislative, and judicial. The executive branch includes both a president and a prime minister. The prime minister is elected by the people. The president is elected by the parliament for a five-year term. The president also appoints cabinet members who work as part of the executive branch.

Greece's legislative branch, or parliament, includes 300 members, who are elected for four-year terms. Voters can choose from among a variety of political parties. The two main ones are the New Democracy Party and the Panhellenic Socialist Movement, known as PASOK.

The judicial branch is headed by the Hellenic Supreme Court of Civil and Penal Law. It consists of 56 judges, who are appointed by the Supreme Judicial Council. After a two-year probationary period, the judges remain in their positions for the rest of their lives if they so desire.[3]

CHAPTER 5
Moving Forward, Slowly

George Papandreou wasn't the only one to blame for the Greek financial crisis. By the time he came into power in 2009, the bulk of the financial mess had already been created. And it seemed it was too late for him to clean it up. The country needed the European Union's help if it was to survive the disaster. But Papandreou and the EU disagreed on the details of how they should move forward.

The prime minister wanted to hold a referendum on the offer that the EU was making the nation. This vote would put the decision on the agreement up to the people of Greece. "Greek people had to feel like they owned the program," Papandreou said, "that it wasn't an imposed program . . . We had to make a decision. We had to decide whether we wanted the program or not, whether we wanted to stay in the euro or not, whether that would have consequences."[1]

The prime minister thought the vote would be a success. "I was very optimistic that the Greek people

Economist Lucas D. Papademos, vice president of the European Central Bank, became Greece's interim prime minister in November of 2011. He served until the following June, when Antonis Samaras assumed the office following a general election.

would have said yes, that it's difficult but we'll go through this [austerity] process, whatever it takes," he said. "And this is why I was so unhappy that there were some negative reactions in Europe."[2]

When he realized that the EU stood firmly against a referendum, Papandreou agreed to step aside. A new coalition government would replace him in leading the country. It would be made up of both PASOK and New Democracy members. They appointed economist Lucas Papademos as interim prime minister. He would serve in the position until elections could be held the following June.

Papandreou would no longer be leading Greece's government. But this didn't mean he wouldn't have a role in it. The country's constitution grants all former prime ministers a seat in Parliament. He would now represent Achaia, a district in southern Greece. He had started out in politics there 30 years earlier.

The people of Greece were divided on how they felt about the situation. Many hated the idea of austerity, the name given to the strict policies that the EU wanted to impose on the country. At the same time, an overwhelming number of Greek citizens wanted to remain a part of the EU. They understood that continuing this membership would come at a price and thought it would be worth it.

Some Greeks saw the situation as an opportunity to start over. Typical was George Pappas, a voter who was fed up with the actions of the country's government. "I'm going to vote for the craziest and least appropriate person this time," he insisted. "I'm beginning to believe that the only way to help this country is to demolish the whole system and start from scratch—even if it means that we leave the eurozone."[3]

Papandreou admitted that big mistakes had been made, and that a new beginning was what was needed. "The slogan that came out almost spontaneously from the people and from our party in 2009 was that either we change or we sink," he pointed out in a 2012 interview. "I still say this today, and I'm even more convinced today, that we were a mismanaged society led by mismanaging governments."[4]

One of the biggest problems Greece was facing was tax evasion, or the illegal nonpayment of taxes. At the same time that the government was spending so much, it wasn't collecting even a fraction of what it should have. A government that doesn't enforce its tax laws has little hope of paying its bills, even when spending is in line.

Ironically, many of the worst offenders were politicians. The mayor of Thessaloniki (Greece's second-largest city), the leader of the Greek national statistical agency, and several former cabinet members were charged with tax evasion after Papandreou's resignation. New laws have made it possible to arrest anyone who owes the government more than 10,000 euros. If a person doesn't pay the amount owed at this time, he or she can be put in jail.

Greece has a long way to go in collecting the taxes it is owed. Estimates place the total amount of tax money the country is owed at 55 billion euros (76 billion dollars). Just 1,500 people owe 13 billion euros ($18 billion) of this debt.[5]

The biggest challenge that the government faces may be getting the people of Greece to pay their taxes from this point forward. Without this revenue, the country has little chance of making it through this crisis. But old habits are hard to break.

George Samothrakis is a tax accountant in Athens. He doesn't think that change in this area will happen quickly. But he also knows that the government needs the money. "I'm afraid it will take several generations to change the mentality here that it is better to not pay your taxes. But because that mentality can't be changed right now," he added, "the government is doing

By 2013, Greece had only collected 19 million euros ($26 million) of the 13 billion euros ($18 billion) due from the 1,500 citizens who owe the most taxes.[7]

whatever it can to increase collection. This is our last chance to get it right."[6]

Another problem that has arisen from the high number of people committing tax evasion is the cost of keeping them in prison. Kostas Karagounis is Greece's deputy justice minister. He thinks that people who owe taxes should be able to turn over their property to the government instead of serving time. Not everyone agrees with this idea. Many think that it allows the rich an unfair advantage. Karagounis thinks that the country needs to focus more on improving its situation. "We have to punish the people who made the mess," he agreed. "But I want them to pay what they owe, more than I want them in jail."[8]

Even with the hope of a new beginning, however, Greece's problems are far from over. It quickly became obvious that the first bailout, totaling $140 billion, was not enough. A second bailout followed in 2012. This one added another $130 billion to the country's national debt. Before it would agree to the second helping of rescue money, the European Union insisted that Greece's government make some major changes. Among them were severe spending cuts, increased taxes, and reform to both its labor and retirement policies.[9]

Government employees in Greece have been soaking up a big part of the country's lavish spending. The perks of working for the government in the past included bonuses for showing up to work on time, Christmas bonuses equal to an entire year's pay, and early retirement complete with generous pensions. Before the crisis, the retirement age in the country was just 53, while in other countries it is considerably higher.[10]

Neither Greece nor the EU has given up hope that the country can reach its new goals. The current plan estimates that the

From 2010 to 2012, Greece became the recipient of the largest bailout in European Union history.[11]

Many Greeks disagreed with the way the government was handling the debt crisis. Massive protests in June 2011 near Greece's parliament turned violent as demonstrators battled police. Hundreds were hospitalized, many with respiratory problems from tear gas.

country's national debt will be reduced to 124 percent of its GDP by 2020. This number is still a far cry from where it needs to be. But just as the mess didn't happen overnight, it also won't be solved quickly.

People around the world are watching Greece as it deals with this crisis. Many think it is unlikely that the country will live up to its new obligations. But Prime Minister Antonis Samaras, who was elected in 2012, chose to focus on his country's progress instead of its past failures. "We are taking steps that show that things have changed in Greece," he declared soon after his election. "We have decreased the salaries of everybody who partakes in politics, from the president to the prime minister to the MPs [members of Parliament]. We have cut expenditures that have to do with Parliament. Everybody knows we are serious."[12]

Greek Prime Minister Antonis Samaras took office in June 2012. In an interesting coincidence, he and George Papandreou were roommates in the early 1970s when they attended Amherst College in Massachusetts. They eventually became bitter political rivals.

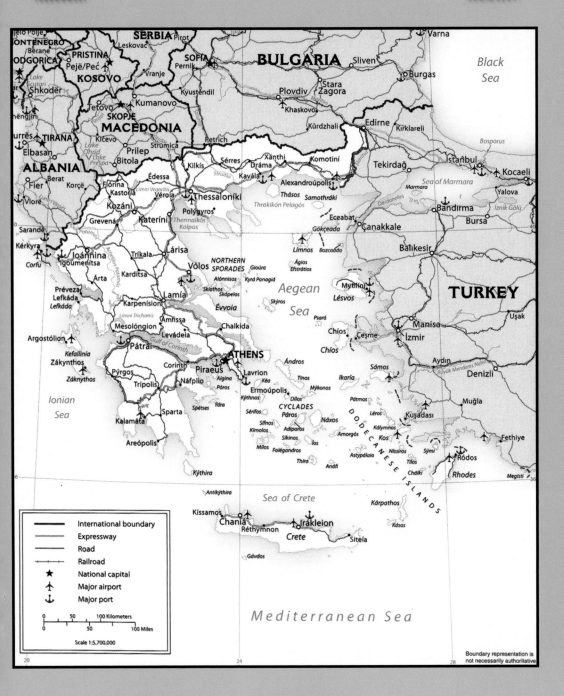

TIMELINE

DATES BCE

ca. 700	Most Greek city-states are ruled by oligarchies.
507	Cleisthenes institutes *demokratia* in Athens.
460	Pericles rises to power and the Golden Age begins.
431	Athens goes to war against Sparta, beginning the Peloponnesian War.
429	Pericles dies during the plague.
413	Syracuse crushes an invading Athenian force.
404	Athens surrenders to Sparta, ending the Peloponnesian War.
338	King Philip II of Macedon defeats the city-states of Greece.
336	King Philip is assassinated; his son Alexander rises to power.
331	Alexander the Great defeats Persia.
323	Alexander dies and the Hellenistic Age begins.
146	Greece becomes a Roman province.
30	The Hellenistic Age ends.

DATES CE

1832	Greeks defeat the Ottoman Turks in the Greek War of Independence.
1896	Athens hosts the first modern Olympic Games.
1924	Greece abolishes its monarchy and becomes a republic.
1935	Greece restores its monarchy.
1941	German troops occupy Greece during World War II.
1944	German forces withdraw from Greece; Georgios Papandreou becomes prime minister.
1946	A civil war begins and lasts for three years.
1952	Greece ratifies its new constitution and becomes a kingdom ruled by parliamentary democracy.
1967	The Greek military stages a coup and takes over the government.
1975	Greece becomes a parliamentary republic with some executive powers given to a president.
1981	Andreas Papandreou becomes prime minister and oversees Greece's admittance to the European Union.
2001	Greece joins the eurozone.
2004	Athens hosts Olympic Games; European Commission issues warning to Greece for falsifying budget data.
2009	George Papandreou becomes prime minister; Greece's credit rating is downgraded as news of financial crisis spreads.
2010	The first bailout from the EU takes place and the Greek government announces austerity measures.
2011	Greece's credit rating is downgraded again; Papandreou resigns.
2012	Second bailout occurs.
2013	The government shuts down public television network ERT without notice as an economy measure, and launches new network EDT.
2014	Prime Minister Antonis Samaras announces that Greece will leave the bailout program this year, with no need for a third aid package.

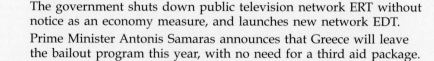

CHAPTER NOTES

Chapter 1: A Greek Tragedy
1. "Greek PM George Papandreou makes farewell address." BBC News, November 9, 2011. http://www.bbc.co.uk/news/world-europe-15655459
2. "Greek vote in early Dec, but no loans until then." CBS News, November 2, 2011. http://www.cbsnews.com/8301-202_162-20128910greek-vote-in-early-dec-but-no-loans-until-then/?pageNum=2
3. David Gow, "Eurozone crisis: banks agree 50% reduction on Greece's debt." *The Guardian*, October 27, 2011. http://www.theguardian.com/world/2011/oct/27/eurozone-crisis-banks-50-greece
4. "Greek vote," CBS News.
5. Derek Gatopoulos, "Did 2004 Olympics spark Greek financial crisis?" *USA Today*, June 3, 2010. http://usatoday30.usatoday.com/sports/olympics/2010-06-03-3222710772_x.htm
6. Ibid.
7. Ibid.
8. 2004 Athens Summer Olympics Fast Facts, CNN. http://www.cnn.com/2013/10/01/world/europe/2004-athens-summer-olympics-fast-facts/
9. "Eurozone crisis explained." BBC, November 27, 2012. http://www.bbc.co.uk/news/business-13798000
10. Dan Alexander, "The World's Largest Debtor Governments, 2013." Forbes.com, November 8, 2013. http://www.forbes.com/sites/danalexander/2013/11/08/worlds-largest-debtor-governments-2013/

Chapter 2: The Birth of Democracy
1. "Ancient Greek Democracy," History.com. http://www.history.com/topics/ancient-greece-democracy
2. Ibid.

Chapter 3: The Golden Ruler
1. "The Greeks – Pericles," PBS. http://www.pbs.org/empires/thegreeks/characters/pericles_p6.html
2. "The Greeks: Crucible of Civilization," PBS. http://www.pbs.org/empires/thegreeks/htmlver/characters/f_pericles.html
3. Ibid.
4. Ibid.
5. Werner Riess, *Performing Interpersonal Violence: Court, Curse, and Comedy in Fourth-Century BCE Athens* (Boston, MA: Walter de Gruyter, 2012), p. 38.
6. Sarah Boseley, "Scientists solve puzzle of death of Pericles." *The Guardian*, January 24, 2006. http://www.theguardian.com/science/2006/jan/24/uknews

Chapter 4: Centuries of Changes
1. "The Four Oxen and the Lion," *Aesop's Fables*. Great Books Online, Bartleby.com http://www.bartleby.com/17/1/52.html
2. "Alexander the Great," History.com http://www.history.com/topics/alexander-the-great
3. "Greece," *The CIA World Factbook* https://www.cia.gov/library/publications/the-world-factbook/geos/gr.html

Chapter 5: Moving Forward, Slowly
1. Joanna Kakissis, "After the Fall: Greece's Former Prime Minister Assesses the State of His Nation." *Time*, May 1, 2012. http://content.time.com/time/world/article/0,8599,2113624,00.html
2. Ibid.
3. Ibid.
4. Ibid.
5. Thomas Landon, "Greek Crackdown on Tax Evasion Yields Little Revenue." *New York Times*, May 12, 2013. http://www.nytimes.com/2013/05/13/business/global/greek-tax-crackdown-yields-little-revenue.html?_r=0
6. Ibid.
7. "Greece Didn't Collect 99.86% of Big Tax Debts." *Greek Reporter*, March 16, 2013. http://greece.greekreporter.com/2013/03/16/greece-didnt-collect-99-86-of-big-tax-debts/
8. Landon, "Greek Crackdown."
9. "Eurozone crisis explained." BBC, November 27, 2012. http://www.bbc.co.uk/news/business-13798000
10. Dianne Francis, "Greece is Not a Country, It's a Party." *Huffington Post*, June 8, 2011. http://www.huffingtonpost.com/diane-francis/greece-is-not-a-country-i_b_871296.html
11. Michael Birnbaum, "Deal reached on $170 billion Greek bailout." *Washington Post*, February 20, 2012. http://www.washingtonpost.com/world/europe/greek-bailout-discussions-stretch-into-tuesday/2012/02/20/gIQASIP4PR_story.html
12. Lally Weymouth, "An interview with Antonis Samaras, Greek prime minister, on austerity and unrest." *Washington Post*, September 14, 2012. http://articles.washingtonpost.com/2012-09-14opinions/35497114_1_troika-report-euro-zone-emergency-liquidity-assistance-program

FURTHER READING

Books

Bensinger, Henry. *Ancient Greek Government*. New York: PowerKids Press, 2013.

Heinrichs, Ann. *Greece*. Danbury, Connecticut: Children's Press, 2012.

Hunt, Jilly. *Greece*. Chicago: Heinemann-Raintree, 2012.

Helfand, Lewis. *400 BC: The Story of the Ten Thousand: A Graphic Novel*. Laurel, MD: Campfire Graphic Novels, 2011.

Wilhelm, Doug. *Alexander the Great: Master of the Ancient World*. Danbury, CT: Franklin Watts, 2010.

Works Consulted

2004 Athens Summer Olympics Fast Facts, CNN. http://www.cnn.com/2013/10/01/world/europe/2004-athens-summer-olympics-fast-facts/

Alexander, Dan. "The World's Largest Debtor Governments, 2013." Forbes.com, November 8, 2013. http://www.forbes.com/sites/danalexander/2013/11/08/worlds-largest-debtor-governments-2013/

Ancient Greek Democracy, History.com. http://www.history.com/topics/ancient-greece-democracy

Birnbaum, Michael. "Deal reached on $170 billion Greek bailout." *Washington Post*, February 20, 2012. http://www.washingtonpost.com/world/europe/greek-bailout-discussions-stretch-into-tuesday/2012/02/20/gIQASIP4PR_story.html

Boseley, Sarah. "Scientists solve puzzle of death of Pericles." *The Guardian*, January 24, 2006. http://www.theguardian.com/science/2006/jan/24/uknews.

"Eurozone crisis explained." BBC News, November 27, 2012. http://www.bbc.co.uk/news/business-13798000.

Francis, Dianne. "Greece is Not a Country, It's a Party." *Huffington Post*, June 8, 2011. http://www.huffingtonpost.com/diane-francis/greece-is-not-a-country-i_b_871296.html

Gatopoulos, Derek. "Did 2004 Olympics spark Greek financial crisis?" *USA Today*, June 3, 2010. http://usatoday30.usatoday.com/sports/olympics/2010-06-03-3222710772_x.htm

Gow, David. "Eurozone crisis: banks agree 50% reduction on Greece's debt." *The Guardian*, October 27, 2011. http://www.theguardian.com/world/2011/oct/27/eurozone-crisis-banks-50-greece

FURTHER READING

"Greece," *The CIA World Factbook*. https://www.cia.gov/library/publications/the-world-factbook/geos/gr.html

"Greece Didn't Collect 99.86% Of Big Tax Debts." *Greek Reporter*, March 16, 2013. http://greece.greekreporter.com/2013/03/16/greece-didnt-collect-99-86-of-big-tax-debts/

"Greek PM George Papandreou makes farewell address." BBC News, November 9, 2011. http://www.bbc.co.uk/news/world-europe-15655459

"Greek vote in early Dec, but no loans until then." CBS News, November 2, 2011. http://www.cbsnews.com/8301-202_162-20128910/greek-vote-in-early-dec-but-no-loans-until-then/?pageNum=2

"The Greeks: Crucible of Civilization." PBS. http://www.pbs.org/empires/thegreeks/htmlver/characters/f_pericles.html

"The Greeks – Pericles," PBS. http://www.pbs.org/empires/thegreeks/characters/pericles_p6.html

Kakissis, Joanna. "After the Fall: Greece's Former Prime Minister Assesses the State of His Nation." *Time*, May 1, 2012. http://content.time.com/time/world/article/0,8599,2113624,00.html

Landon, Thomas. "Greek Crackdown on Tax Evasion Yields Little Revenue." *New York Times*, May 12, 2013. http://www.nytimes.com/2013/05/13/business/global/greek-tax-crackdown-yields-little-revenue.html?_r=0

Manolopoulos, Jason. *Greece's 'Odious' Debt*. New York: Anthem Press, 2011.

Riess, Werner. *Performing Interpersonal Violence: Court, Curse, and Comedy in Fourth-Century BCE Athens*. Boston, MA: Walter de Gruyter, 2012.

Spielvogel, Jackson J. *Western Civilization: A Brief History, Volume I*. Boston, MA, Wadsworth, 2010.

Weymouth, Lally. "An interview with Antonis Samaras, Greek prime minister, on austerity and unrest." *Washington Post*, September 14, 2012. http://articles.washingtonpost.com/2012-09-14/opinions/35497114_1_troika-report-euro-zone-emergency-liquidity-assistance-program

GLOSSARY

abolish (uh-BAHL-ish) — To put an end to; eliminate.

assassinate (uh-SASS-uh-neyt) — To kill suddenly or secretly, especially a politically prominent person.

austerity (aw-STEHR-uh-tee) — Reduced spending and increased emphasis on saving.

default (dee-FAWLT) — The failure to meet financial obligations.

etymology (eh-tuh-MAHL-uh-jee) — The origin of a word.

infrastructure (IN-fruh-struhk-cher) — The fundamental facilities and systems of an area such as a city.

oligarchy (AHL-uh-gahr-kee) — A form of government in which all power is vested in a few persons or a dominant class.

oppress (uh-PRESS) — To burden with cruel or unjust impositions or restraints.

ostracize (OS-truh-size) — To banish a person from his or her native country

pension (PEN-shuhn) — A fixed amount of money paid at regular intervals beginning when someone retires.

recession (ree-SESH-uhn) — A period of economic contraction.

tax evasion (TAKS ee-VAY-zhuhn) — The deliberate nonpayment of taxes.

PHOTO CREDITS: All design elements from Thinkstock/Sharon Beck; Cover—pp. 1, 21, 22, 23, 27—Thinkstock; p. 5—Vasileios Filis/AFP/Getty Images/Newscom; p. 8—Wu Wei/ZUMAPRESS/Newscom; p. 11—Stefan Matzke/ZUMAPRESS/Newscom; p. 13—Album/Prisma/Newscom; p. 14—Design Pics/Newscom; p. 15—Ohio State House; p. 16—akg-images/Peter Connolly/Newscom; pp. 19, 28, 39—cc-by-sa; p. 24—akg-images/Newscom; p. 30—Louisa Gouliamaki/Getty Images; p. 31—Library of Congress, LC-USZ62-94148; p. 32—Roger Viollet/Getty Images; p. 35—Wiktor Dabkowski/ZUMApress/Newscom; p. 40—Alexandros Vlachos/EPA/Newscom; p. 41—The University of Texas at Austin, Perry-Castañeda Library Map Collection.

INDEX

About the Author

Tammy Gagne is the author of numerous books for adults and children, including three other titles in the Evolution of Government and Politics series for Mitchell Lane Publishers. One of her favorite pastimes is visiting schools to talk to kids about the writing process.